Animals of the World

Komodo Dragon

By Edana Eckart

Children's Press®
A Division of Scholastic Inc.
New York / Toronto / London / Auckland / Sydney
Mexico City / New Delhi / Hong Kong
Danbury, Connecticut

Photo Credits: Cover © Stuart Westmorland/Corbis; pp. 5, 9, 17, 19, 21 © Wolfgang Kaehler/Corbis; p. 7 © W. Perry Conway/Corbis; p. 11 Photo by Jessie Cohen, National Zoological Park © Smithsonian Institution; p. 13 © Michael Pitts/Nature Picture Library; p. 15 © Premaphotos/Animals Animals
Contributing Editor: Jennifer Silate
Book Design: Mindy Liu

Library of Congress Cataloging-in-Publication Data

Eckart, Edana.
    Komodo dragon / by Edana Eckart.
    p. cm.—(Animals of the world)
    Includes index.
    Summary: An introduction to the physical characteristics and behavior of the komodo dragon, the largest lizard on Earth.
    ISBN 0-516-24295-4 (lib. bdg.)—ISBN 0-516-27893-2 (pbk.)
    1. Komodo dragon—Juvenile literature. [1. Komodo dragon. 2. Lizards.] I. Title. II. Series.

QL666.L29 E35 2003
597.95'968—dc21

                                                              2002153944

Contents

The **Komodo dragon** is the largest **lizard** on Earth.

5

Komodo dragons have very long tails.

They also have short legs.

Komodo dragons have long **tongues**, too.

Komodo dragons lay eggs.

Their babies are inside
the eggs.

The eggs are very big.

Young Komodo dragons live in trees most of the time.

They live there to be safe from other Komodo dragons.

13

Komodo dragons eat **deer** and other animals.

15

Komodo dragons eat together.

17

Many Komodo dragons live on Komodo **Island**.

18

People come to Komodo Island to see the Komodo dragon.

Komodo dragons are **amazing** animals.

21

New Words

amazing (uh-**maze**-ing) very surprising

deer (**dihr**) animals with four long legs and short, brown fur

island (**eye**-luhnd) a piece of land that has water all around it

Komodo dragon (kuh-**moh**-doh **drag**-uhn) a very large lizard

lizard (**liz**-urd) a reptile with a scaly body, four legs, and a long tail

tongues (**tuhngz**) long parts that move inside animals' mouths

To Find Out More

Books
Amazing Lizards
by Trevor Smith
Econo-Clad Books

Komodo Dragons
by Louise Martin
Rourke Enterprises

Web Site
Enchanted Learning: Komodo Dragon
http://www.enchantedlearning.com/subjects/reptiles/lizard/
   Komodoprintout.shtml
Learn about the Komodo dragon and color a picture of one
on this Web site.

Index

About the Author
Edana Eckart has written several children's books. She enjoys bike riding with her family.

Reading Consultants
Kris Flynn, Coordinator, Small School District Literacy, The San Diego County Office of Education

Shelly Forys, Certified Reading Recovery Specialist, W.J. Zahnow Elementary School, Waterloo, IL

Sue McAdams, Former President of the North Texas Reading Council of the IRA, and Early Literacy Consultant, Dallas, TX